I BELIEVE
MY TESTIMONY OF
YESHUA
JESUS THE MESSIAH

I BELIEVE
MY TESTIMONY OF
YESHUA
JESUS THE MESSIAH

JULIA PERANIO MS

Xulon Press
2301 Lucien Way #415
Maitland, FL 32751
407.339.4217
www.xulonpress.com

© 2022 by Julia Peranio MS

All rights reserved solely by the author. The author guarantees all contents are original and do not infringe upon the legal rights of any other person or work. No part of this book may be reproduced in any form without the permission of the author.

Due to the changing nature of the Internet, if there are any web addresses, links, or URLs included in this manuscript, these may have been altered and may no longer be accessible. The views and opinions shared in this book belong solely to the author and do not necessarily reflect those of the publisher. The publisher therefore disclaims responsibility for the views or opinions expressed within the work.

Unless otherwise indicated, Scripture quotations taken from the King James Version (KJV) – *public domain*.

Paperback ISBN-13: 978-1-66285-075-2
Ebook ISBN-13: 978-1-66285-076-9

Table of Contents

My First Miracle – The White Slippers 1
The Addiction 5
My Daughter was Gay 13
The Birth of My Son 29
The Holy Presence of God 35
The Book – A Principle of Faith 41
The Death of My Father 45
An Ill-Fated Flight 51
The Deceptive Engagement 55
Home 61
The Trip to Israel 67
The Poem 71
A Partner 77

Introduction — Why I am Writing this Book

My reason for writing this book is simple. For a long time, I have needed to say something that is relevant to everyone. In the past, I wrote short articles and poems in periodicals and books of poetry. Even though I got to see my words in print, I never felt accomplished, because I knew there were more realities lurking inside me waiting to be released in the form of a book. Each trial and testing I experienced taught me something different, which I can pass on to others. I have the gift of sharing which I enjoy doing. I could not understand why I felt so much pleasure making others happy through sharing. I was told that it was a blessing and a gift from God. Now I wish to share my testimonies of God's grace and mercies with you in the hope that it will help you.

The incidences are not unique. Many individuals have had similar events, but writing a book allowed me to impart my personal experiences to you on a wider scale. Others can learn and grow through seeing how Yeshua miraculously brought me out of each situation. We have all lived through numerous circumstances and trials, some more than others. Problems can impact our jobs, homes, communities, and societies. No one is exempt; there is a real enemy at work, one who never gets tired or disinterested in destroying lives. God has said in His Word – "Seek me and you will find me" (Jer. 29:13). "I am as close as your breath" (Job 33:4). David declared that the Lord was his strength and his shield in (Ps. 28:7). Who else can cover and protect us like God? Believe me, when I tell you that the battle has already been won. Just stand your ground in Christ and in peace be still. You will see how He comes through for you.

My experiences have been supernatural; I have had so many since childhood, and now it is time to share some of them with you. As you read, please pray that God will open the portals of heaven and bless you with love, knowledge, and understanding. He will teach you how to war in your spirit and to become a conqueror. Today, focus on His words, taking a daily dosage. My mind is steady, and my spirit is lifted. Being a child of God is my success story. I did not get here overnight. I had to press into God in a determined way, purposefully moving to the mark of the high calling. I learned to claim His promises and feed them into my life's situations. Navigating the Bible allows for supernatural knowledge and application, which can only be received through the workings of the Holy Spirit.

At this point, I aim to convey what God has done for me and show how He can do the same for you. The circumstances felt like mountains, and trying to solve them through my efforts brought me additional pain. The good news is that I applied the formula "Believe in the Lord Jesus Christ and he shall be saved" (Acts 16:31). In our lives, we make mistakes and pay for them dearly. Sometimes the devil attacks randomly, catching us off guard. Whatever the situation, use the above formula. I came to realize that with God there is hope. He will turn you around, strengthen you and set you on the right path. Living

At this point, I aim to convey what God has done for me and show how He can do the same for you. The circumstances felt like mountains, trying to solve them through my efforts brought me additional pain. The good news is that I applied the formula "Believe in the Lord Jesus Christ and he shall be saved" (Acts 16:31). In our lives, we make mistakes and pay for them dearly. Sometimes the devil attacks randomly, catching us off guard. Whatever the situation, use the above formula. I came to realize that with God there is hope. He will turn you around, strengthen you and set you on the right path. Living blindly, there are no guarantees; one becomes vulnerable to the wiles of the devil. We leave ourselves open to destruction and death, with no place to turn in our disobedience. The needless sufferings we encounter are a result of our own rebellion, as we struggle to find meaning in a world lost in the age of the self. God's plan of salvation is made ready and available to those who are willing to get out of the fight and find peace, a shalom in Yeshua. It is time to take hold of life and real living through the blood of the Lamb. He will teach you and bring you into all truth (John 16:13).

This book is called "I Believe – My testimonies of Yeshua Jesus the Messiah" I gave it this name because of the experiences I have had where God miraculously came through for me. He showed Himself to me on so many different occasions therefore I believe in Him and the incidences are my testimony. It will show you how loving Jehovah God is and how He keeps His promises. When I cried out to Him making known my troubles and trials, He extended open arms to help me. It will show you how He came through at the right time. My faith was not strong, but I believed He would save me if I called upon Him. You will learn to keep your eyes on God the restorer, healer, father, and friend. You will understand how concentrating on the problem breeds fear and doom, which will take away all light and hope. Trouble will come, that's for sure; but hold on to His unflinching hand. I hope when you are finished reading this book, you will be blessed knowing that God can do the same and more wondrous things for you. Here are some questions for you. "Have you been grafted into the vine?" and "What about your prayer life?" Let's not wait until our backs are against the wall before seeking Him. Staying in the Word will keep you ready to face any battle. You will be firm, fearless, and strong in the faith to fight the good fight. Remember to "Trust in the Lord with all your heart and lean not unto your own understanding; but in all thy ways acknowledge Him and he will direct your path" (Prov. 3:5-6). "May the Lord bless you and keep you, the Lord make His face shine upon you, and be gracious unto you. The Lord lifts up His countenance upon you and gives you peace." (Numbers 6:24-26).

First Miracle – The White Slippers

My father had a passion for animals; he loved dogs and birds, which he raised at home. We grew up playing among chickens, pigeons, and turkeys, as they ran about the yard. We mimicked their sounds and enjoyed learning about the animals first hand. Of course, we ate well especially on Saturdays and Sundays, as father always had a few prepared for weekend dinners. During the week-days, we had fresh eggs. My mother cooked well but my father was the chef. He loved fishing and he taught us all to fish. Today it is my favorite past time.

The animals were lovely, but they pooped everywhere. It was my older brother's duty to clean up after the dogs. The birds and chickens roamed about and we had to be careful not the step in the wrong places, especially since we did not have extra shoes for wearing outside. I was not so careful. I might have been six or seven years old at the time. Walking bare-footed was a bother,

I often had to clean my feet with small sticks lying about. This time I had enough, I knew my parents could not afford to purchase shoes just for that, so I decided to ask Father God to provide for me. I stand amazed at the trust I had in Him at such a tender age; yet it wavered as I grew older. I remembered talking to God about the chicken poop and stepping in the mess and how it felt disgusting going between my toes.

Talking to God like that was so personal, we had a good relationship. I could not have understood what that meant at such a tender age. He is a personal God who wants to be with us, helping and caring for us at all times. Nothing is too big or too small for God. The innocence I had astonishes me to this day. I was sure that God would hear me and answer my request. I remembered this incident taking place in the cool of the day. I was sitting by a tree on a big stone thinking about my life and how to counteract the bird poop dilemma. I was wearing a white dress with a broken zipper and I was bare-footed with brownish dirt all over my feet. I told God my situation and what I wanted. I was very detailed, I asked Him for a pair of white slippers with cut −work flowers for the design. The slippers must be able to slip on and off the back of my heel and have a shiny buckle to the side. When I was done, I felt a sense of relief knowing that they would be coming soon. The excitement was overwhelming, I did not tell a soul as it was between me and God.

One day I was at home playing with my brothers and my mother came home and called me to come in doors. I was not too happy leaving the fun we were having, and went on the second call. She quickly opened a shopping bag and took out a narrow box and gave it to me. I started to open the box and what I saw inside confounded me; I was frozen for a few seconds. It was the pair of white slippers I requested of God, He heard me and listened to my every word. The slippers were exactly as I had described them. I could not believe my eyes. This was months after my request, I had forgotten about my talk with God, but He remembered me. As young as I was, He treated me like there was no one else more precious or important than me. I still could not believe what happened. Being a child, I quietly went to my mother and asked her this question. "Mom did you hear me when I was praying to God for these slippers?" and she said, "Child, go and sit down." I thought she might have heard my prayers; but she did not, It was all God. I thanked her for purchasing the shoes and walked away thanking God for answering my prayers. When God was making me, He was thinking of me alone. When He was making you, he had only you on His mind. We are special to Him, He sees us as individuals. When He died on the cross, you were on His mind, and I was on His mind too. So you see, He is a personal God, one who hears and listens when we cry, when we pray. Trust Him to be your everything and you won't be disappointed.

"All good and perfect gifts comes from above" (James 1:17) and "without faith, it is impossible to please God" (Hebrews 11:16). Furthermore, "God wants to give us the desire of our hearts." (Psalm 37:4). He wants to please us and make us happy. So "Ask, seek, knock and it shall be given to you" (Matthew 7:7-8). However, we must remember to "seek first the kingdom of God and His righteousness and all these thing shall be added unto you" (Matthew 7:7-12). This miracle stayed with me because it was the first one I can remember clearly and knew quite early that God answers prayer.

The Addiction

Many people know what they want to be at an early age. I didn't when it came to my career goals — I was lost. God has a plan for us, and we must put Him first in our lives. The Savior will guide us and teach us all things. Life has a way of captivating our attention, and the enemy of our souls comes to steal and destroy. Being talented as a child, I hoped that as I matured my career goals would become clearer. Everyone in my family seemed to be moving towards their educational interest except me. Later in life, my mother became a professional and worked as a nurse at Andrews Hospital in Kingston, Jamaica. She was good at her job. I knew immediately that the medical field was not my calling. My father was a mechanic with other electrical skills in the automotive field. I remembered asking him to teach me the skill of building car batteries from scratch, as this was very interesting to me. He flat out refused, and told me that I was a female and this field was geared toward men. Two of my older brothers went into that automotive field. The eldest went for agriculture and another brother went into the construction industry. My youngest brother has a chronic illness so he never worked, and my sister who is younger than me went into the medical field. I thought she was heading towards education and becoming a teacher. I say this because she stayed at school with her little friends all day during summer breaks. The neighborhood children attended her home academy.

In high school, I veered towards business, learning some accounting, typewriting, shorthand and took some business courses. I wanted to do bigger and better things, but I just didn't know what to do. When I graduated from secretarial school, I worked as a sales representative at a small stationary company. I left that job after one year and went to cosmetology school for almost two years. Before graduating, I quit after losing interest in the subject. I then went into banking and worked in the city at one of the well-established banks in Jamaica as an account's clerk. Working in that field felt good for a while, I dressed professionally every day and enjoyed meeting and helping people. I stayed at the bank job for two months before migrating to the United States.

Coming to America, my whole career concept changed. There were so many different areas of study from which to choose. I was immediately drawn to electronics, I knew exactly what I wanted to do. The irresistible commercials detailing the different schools and the curriculum pertaining to electronics fascinated me. I wanted to work on the dashboard of planes, repair computers, work in hydrolysis, robotics, and build programs…I was ready to go.

Seven months after migrating, I was adapting to the new system and acquainting myself to a new country. I chose to attend the local technical college. I was in for a big surprise when I started school. I was the only female in most of my classes, and before long I was the only one. The institution was predominantly male-oriented; no one had informed me of this fact. If someone had told me, I would have been better prepared and probably would have handled myself differently. In those days, a female could study in different male-dominated fields; however, it could prove difficult to navigate or get employment.

To this day I still feel that I was way ahead of my time. The courses were challenging, but I excelled and tried not to be intimidated and maintained a good attitude. Growing up with five brothers helped a lot. I dealt with male dominance, gave respect, and got it back in return. Break time, however, was desertion. I sat alone every day and got a few hellos, but that was it. I wanted to fit in and hoped that they would accept, or see me as one of the guys. They would all go to the back of the building or gather around a big tree outside at picnic tables. I was not brave enough to join them without being invited. One day a young man called me over to chat with him. He was smoking a cigarette. I was hesitant but glad for the opportunity to ultimately have a friend at school.

We met every break time and soon other guys joined our table, they all smoked. One afternoon my friend asked me to have a smoke. I refused, but went to the pool hall to play darts and drink a beer. I was having fun being friends with them and deep down I knew there was some compromise; but I figured it would do no harm. When I think back on what I did, the story of Lot comes to mind. He pitched his tent towards Sodom (Genesis 13:12). He did not go right away; but sure enough, that's where he ended up.

There were two young men who looked at me differently. They never joined our group, and I felt they were trying to tell me something; but were not willing to interfere. We were on break and headed for the outdoors when three of my friends handed me a cigarette and I took it. Without a care in the world, I started puffing. I started fitting in and the men accepted me. It felt great. I even had my favorite brand of cigarettes, which were harsh and stronger than most of the guy's brands. I was living with my parents at the time. My mother complained about the smell for cigarettes on my clothes. I would lie about it. I had the best alibi, the men at school smoked and I could not help being in the environment. My mother suspected that I was smoking, she was clever. I was not sure though, so I decided to be discreet and more careful about her actually finding out.

It was close to finals, and I was happy the two-year course was coming to an end. The guys asked if I wanted to go with them to visit one of the friend in our group mother, at her home just to "hang out." Being friends with them, I found it harmless so I agreed to go. It was a large house. I met my friend's mother for the first time and we hit it off immediately. After a few minutes of being there, everyone went to the back-yard. In my mind, we were getting ready for a barbeque or some innocent fun. The guys formed a circle which I joined. At the top of the circle was the mother. She had a weird bottle in her hand with smoke coming from it, and they started passing it around the circle. It was a marijuana pipe, I learned about this later. Everyone was puffing on it, and I was expected to do the same. This time I felt fearful something dark was happening. My heart was racing uncontrollably. I said, "God, what am I going to do now?" I knew I had to draw the line somewhere. I was smoking cigarettes already and hiding it from my family, which was enough. The pipe got closer and the next thing I knew, it was in my hand. I thought to myself *How could a mother do this?* My mother came to mind. She was clean, decent, and God-fearing, a woman of principle who would do nothing of the sort. The time went by slowly as I passed it on to the next person without puffing on it.

A sense of relief came over my whole body, and after they all took puffs, the apparatus was taken back inside. The next fifteen minutes was quiet. She laughed a lot and bid us good-bye until next time. All seven or eight of us drove back to school, where we went our separate ways. The following day it was the usual. At break time, I went to our regular place, and I was by myself. The guys were disappointed in my decision not to use marijuana. They turned their backs on me pretending I was not there. I saw them and they saw me, but no one spoke to me. The reality was they were never my friends. This continued until we graduated. I took pictures with seventy males and was the only female among them. They left and I never saw them again. I compromised everything I believed just because I wanted to make friends with those fellows, and they dropped me like a lead weight. The voracity of what I did and the treatment that followed brought me to my senses. I decided *Okay! Now I have to clean myself up and ask God for forgiveness.* At least I did not smoke pot/marijuana. To some people smoking pot is nothing. I was raised in a good Christian home where I knew God for myself. I've sat and chatted with the Lord many times. He is not a stranger to me. The body temple is precious too and I know better not to smoke period. It is a big deal for me not to dishonor the body temple because "we are not our own our body is a temple" (Corinthians 6:19) and "we are fearfully and wonderfully made" (Psalm 139:14). We have to take care of the body temple and allow the Holy Spirit to live within us. If the devil can get one-third of God's angels, we must understand how clever he is. It is important to never underestimate him. I thought the refusing the marijuana ended everything. Satan knew that the damage was already done. I cleaned myself up and decided never to smoke again. Wrong! I was hooked.

Nicotine addiction is one of the strongest and hardest addictions to break. The need for it was so great that I kept quitting and starting every other week. My desire for smoking was gone, but the addiction held me hostage. I called my aunt Glentine, who lived in Jamaica, and told her about my situation. She informed me of her next visit to the US, which was soon; she said we could be baptized together and renew my walk with God. This seems like a great plan. Surely baptism would take away the addiction. Two weeks later, she came and we went into the water grave of baptism together. I was sure this demonstration of faith would work because my actions would show God how genuine I was. Weeks passed and nothing changed. I felt like a large, heavy chain was placed around my neck. Indeed, this was a heavy yoke. I was in bondage, and I cried to God for help more than once without success. I could not do this on my own. I knew I needed the help of God, not man. Usually, the specialists and professionals' advise wearing the patch or attending NA (Nicotine Addiction) group sessions to assist with the problem. The difference was I had firsthand experience of Yeshua's working power, so those recommendations were not warranted for me. After praying, crying, and trying on my own, I got angry at God for something I did to myself knowing it was wrong. How unfair could I be?

Thank God for His tender mercies. I am glad His love is unconditional and He forgives us of our sins when we are upset and mad at Him. Weeks passed and my struggles continued, until I forgot about the addiction. I did not care anymore. I still went to church; but I was condemned by my actions. I sang in church and acted out the part of the good Christian; but I was biding my time until my next nicotine fix.

One night I went to bed just like any other nights, hiding my cigarettes, cleaning up the smell on my person, and off to sleep. The next thing I knew I was up in the clouds with an angel. We were flying together, only I had no wings. I wondered what I was doing with her, and she heard me even though I did not speak verbally. The angel brought me closer to the earth, and I saw a man. He was the most handsome human being I ever saw; but the look on his face was telling. He appeared to be very concerned, worried, and fearful, with some urgency. He was well dressed as a male model, very shiny shoes, hair properly groomed. I asked the angel who he was. We spoke with our minds telepathically. The angel told me that he was the devil, and I was shocked, because he was well dressed like my good friend who offered me the first cigarette. This part of my encounter with the devil was so real and spiritually enlightning. There I was looking at the devil and his expression, and for the first time I could see him; but he did not have the power to see me. That's how powerful and almighty God is. The angel showed me something else; but I was too high in the air to figure out what it was. Angels can see from any distance. We humans are limited, so we need divine assistance. It seemed like straws that were cut and bound like hay, then the angel took me closer and what I saw blew my mind. It was cigarettes bound together by demon workers getting them ready for distribution. At that moment I thought to myself that I was not in that category and those were not for me. I am not a smoker, the scene was so profound. In that moment I knew the Lord allowed me to feel the displeasure, the vile sin of smoking, and how undesirable it is to the Father. Our body is the temple of the Lord — we are not our own. How could I have done such a wicked thing that displeased God? I remembered my addiction problem while in the vision. Words cannot explain how being placed in that position brought about an eye-opening, realistic experience. This was an angel showing me the wrong I was doing in my body, and in the sight of God. This brought about a rude awakening for me, understanding that I am not my own. Right there in my spirit I knew that if I didn't change, I believed I would be lost forever.

It was so important to God that I quit smoking. He loves me so much; no one will be smoking in heaven. The well-dressed man was the distributor and deceiver Satan himself. That's how sin is; it comes wrapped in fancy paper and pretty bows. Everything became clear as I woke up. For two days I was lost in my mind and in my convictions. I could not stop the thoughts of what I saw, and to my amazement, my addiction was gone. The cravings and urges to smoke were not there anymore. It appeared as though I never smoked and I knew I was healed. It didn't matter if an individual blew smoke in my face. I was cleansed, renewed. God saved me. Blessed be the name of the Lord. He did it again. "Trust in the Lord with all your heart and lean not on your own understanding, but in all your ways acknowledge Him and He will direct your path" (Proverbs 3:5-6).

My Daughter Was Gay

God blessed me with two beautiful children, a boy and a girl. Juliette, my daughter is the older and Datta, my son, the younger. My mother named my daughter after me, and I named my son after the character Data, the droid from Star Trek series. I placed an extra "t" in his name for variation — I was a Trekky. Juliette is a gem, a very precious stone; she is smart, beautiful, and God fearing. What happened to this child is nothing less than a miracle and the very best one yet.

In kindergarten, the school called us to say that she was not keeping up with the rest of the class. My husband, at that time and I went to the school to inquire what was wrong. We were very concerned. We knew she was brilliant from home studies and training. Something had to be causing this problem. Upon arrival at the school, the teachers were reserved and scarcely spoke about the issue. They claimed that Juliette was disengaged and not repeating the alphabet or saying the common words recited each day by other class-mates. Following a brief meeting with the principal, it was decided to have her tested. We got a letter in the mail within a few weeks. The letter stated that Juliette was performing above average and we should consider her for the Magnet program. We took the letter to the principal. The school had received one too. Juliette's class teacher was embarrassed and could not face us because of her incorrect assessment. Juliette started the Magnet program very early and did well in school which was promising. In her early years, age three to four; I noticed shed refused to wear stockings and dresses with pretty laces, like other little girls. At first, I thought she didn't like things on her legs, but she liked socks. Overall, Juliette asked to be dressed like a boy. She ran with the boys and had fun with them. I did not interfere with her because I had been a tom-boy as well, and grew out of that stage. I hoped she would too, but that did not happen.

The good news came when she gave her life to God at the tender age of seven. Our family went to a crusade for four weeks. Pastor Samuels from Jamaica was the evangelist, a fierce and dynamic speaker for the Lord. Upon completion of the crusade, many souls were won for the kingdom, including Juliette's. At the end of the crusade, there was an altar call; Juliette told me that she wanted to be baptized. I did not second guess her because even though she was seven years old, she was spiritual and intelligent. I knew how she felt about God. I walked her to the tent altar and Pastor Samuels came to discuss her decision. He told her that he had twin daughters seven years of age and would not consider baptizing them as they were too young. He said to Juliette, "Convince me why I should baptize you." Juliette looked him in the face, paused and quietly said, "I want to walk in light, not the darkness." He was taken back at her response. It was so insightful. Pastor Samuels turned to me and said. "Mom, get her ready," and she was baptized. Jesus said, "Suffer the little children to come unto me, and forbid them not: for of such is the Kingdom of God. Verily I say unto you, whosoever shall not receive the Kingdom of God as a little child shall in no wise enter therein" (Matthew 19:14). Juliette's statement, "I want to walk in the light, not the darkness," played a pivotal role in her life, as you will see later. I believe God sealed her for Himself that day and nothing could tear her away from the grasp of the Master. During her teenage years, she had many friends, especially girls, but one was special. She came to the house a lot. Many times they would be seen at home together being best friends, or so I thought. By the time my divorce came about, she became withdrawn and reserved. However, Juliette and I remained loving and kind to each other, and she never rebelled. Later in her high school years, I found out that she was counseled for the divorce. In every young girl's life, a boyfriend will show up. Juliette never seemed to have any interest in boys until about twenty years old. A young junior pastor fell for her and asked for her hand in marriage. I was elated because finally, my thoughts of her being gay were incorrect. She was just now ready to date and found one young man attractive enough. In all honesty, I knew that he was afflicted with issues of his own, but I refused to acknowledge that. I saw what was going on in her life; but I refuted it with every fiber of my being. Mothers know their children, especially if they have a great relationship.

The evil one had infiltrated my beautiful God-given gift of a child, Juliette. The cursed demon spirit should not be a part of my family. I questioned myself, from where, and why did it come? The affliction came straight from the pit of hell. This wonderful development proved to be a mirage weaved and concocted to destroy and lead her further into damnation. My daughter got engaged to this young man, he and I went to pick out and purchase the ring. He came to the church which we were attending at that time and familiarized himself with everyone there. This person preached most convincingly, sang beautifully and fellowshipped. He later spent a few days with us before leaving for his home. It was time to meet his side of the family. His father was welcoming. His mother, on the other hand, was a bit reserved. The young man was a student at Oakwood College and had just a few more months to complete his studies. Juliette went to meet with him there so they could figure out where to live following the marriage. I was so happy things appeared to be going in the correct direction.

When Juliette got back from meeting with him, she shared with me her heartfelt feelings. She said, "Mom I cannot marry him, I don't like boys and furthermore, he is not who he pretends to be" she said everything was a lie. My whole world fell apart. I knew something was wrong, but I was not prepared to hear my daughter finally admit and confirm that she was gay. What God-fearing parent wants to accept such a lie? From that time, Juliette started dating women openly. One cannot imagine the depth of my pain and sorrow. I remembered teaching both of my children about Sodom and Gomorrah and how God hated the sin of homosexuality, among other shameful, disgusting, sinful behaviors. The rug was pulled out from under me. I had to fall back on whatever Christian teachings of endurance, faith, love, and long-suffering I had learned; but it was God's grace and mercy that kept me though it all. Everything became clear when I looked back to the days she invited girls home and spent lots of time with them. I was not worried about her getting pregnant prematurely, as she seemed well behaved, proper, and disciplined. In my view, the world changed as I knew it. For the first time I had to seek the meaning of being gay and try to understand my part in the anomaly. When the church got wind of it, they treated her poorly. Their children were not allowed to be around her because she was now contagious. They told me to report her to the pastor and board members so her positions there could be taken away. Now my baby was the devil doomed for hell and her soul was lost forever. I know God did not give me a throwaway child, no sir! So it was time to fight for my daughter's salvation through prayer, fasting, and humility in the spirit. Those Christians who rejected my child were the same ones who were present at her dedication service, when she was born. This was the time when I needed my church brethren the most. I wanted them to stand in the gap and pray with me and for me on behalf of Juliette. "Bear one another's burdens, and so fulfill the Law of Christ" (Galatians 6:2). The rejection was so bad that she left that congregation and started visiting a different church. By this time, she was dating a young lady from the recent congregation and I knew this. I asked her to be respectful of my lifestyle. We lived together in a Christian home. I treated her with the utmost respect and she demonstrated the same to me. Her dates or girlfriends were not expected to be a part of our home. I explained my position to her with love, I told her that while I hated the sin, I loved her; further, the lifestyle she was living went against all the principles of Yeshua. She understood and accepted the terms. Months went by, one afternoon my daughter came home crying and told me that everyone she loved always walked away eventually, including her present girlfriend. My daughter asked me if she could come to my congregation for a change. I was so happy and, although she dressed like a male with a tie, vest and even male shoes, I had to look beyond the outside and reach into her soul with all the understanding and compassion I could muster. I never criticized her or asked her to change her dress code.

God is the only one who can change an individual. Forcing her to be different would have pushed her away, and prove to be counterproductive. Maybe, she would dress like a woman while in church to please me but, what's in her heart? I had to wait patiently and allow God to work on her heart. "A new heart also will I give you, and a new spirit will I put within you: and I will take away the stony heart out of your flesh, and I will give you a heart of flesh. And I will put my spirit within you, and cause you to walk in My Statues, and ye shall keep My judgments, and do them. Without Me you can do nothing" (Ezekiel 36:26-27 and John 15:5).

Some of the congregants from my church glanced at her when she walked in for the first time dressed like a man; but she ignored the looks. I was glad that the relationship with her girlfriend was over and she was seeking the Lord again. I was proud of her, in my mind, it felt like she was no longer gay; but this was wishful thinking. I have a dear friend called Mary who has a heart for the Lord. Her loving kindness is a demonstration of who God is. We met in college while pursuing a graduate program in education. This lady is an educator; God placed her into my life for a reason. When the going got too tough in collage, we stayed together and made it through. Her actions were greater than words can express, this was where I learned about the dedication and faithfulness she possessed. We kept our friendship throughout the years, and when I needed her for my daughter, she was there. I called her up and informed her about Juliette, and how my heart was broken because of her situation. Mary told me that she had a prayer line and that she would mention Juliette's name and her situation to them. Wow! More prayer, more power. That was great; I now had a friend to help in the battle. This is a true friend, God can place people in your life that will pray with you, cry with you, and be happy for you in your success.

People who love the Lord Yeshua give of their services willing to help others. Mary is no exception and I am happy to have her in my life. I call her my praying friend. She understood what I was up against, and it was not easy. The demon and dragon, the accuser of our souls, wanted my child. Now I had a host of Christian believers staying in the fight with me. After a couple of weeks I got a call from Mary, she told me that one of the members saw a demon trying to take my daughter. The demon said to her, "How dare you intercede for her," The lady asked that we continue lifting Juliette up to the Lord.

In less than six months, Juliette's visits to the church became few and far between. I noticed that she was on the internet a lot, and when I walked into her bedroom the computer would go blank. She was engaging in the online dating scene. Eventually she stopped attending church altogether. My faith never wavered. Juliette would be changed. The term, "it's the darkest just before dawn" is a reality. I said it to myself, believing God for deliverance and a miracle. I was invited to a temple call the Mishkan David in Sunrise Florida by a lady named Lilly. She was a member of that messianic congregation. I was standing in a department store window shopping when she called out to me. "Beautiful" she said, three times and I did not answer because I was not sure she was addressing me, finally I turned around after the fourth greeting. She said, "yes you," I need your help in choosing the correct color curtains. Later I saw this was a ruse to invite me to her temple.

We conversed for about an hour, and soon we realized that we had a lot in common. Although she is much older than I am, the age difference was not a factor. It felt like we knew each other for many years. By the time she asked me to visit her church, I was already comfortable to say yes. I went to the very next meeting, a Shabbat morning service. The visit was worshipful, and I had a great time in the Lord. The sermon was very spiritual. The people were friendly, loving and kind. I had to leave early due to a previous engagement, but I wanted to return and continue the visit. My soul was blessed. The speaker and leader Rabbi Gabriel Simkin is a powerful teacher and instructor who practices what he preaches from the Word of God. His wife and praise team leader, Esther Simkin, spiritually leads the congregation into wonderful worship songs and music, lifting each heart heavenwards. I knew immediately that God sent for me through Lilly. He wanted me to experience a deeper, closer spiritual enterprise with Him. The kind of worship that would take me places into the spiritual realm that I had never been before. I have worshipped in the past and felt good, but not like this. Everyone was in unison in the spirit praising God. The Holy Spirit's presence was overwhelming during the praise and worship sessions and sermons. There were no side-bars and the children were controlled lovingly so that there could be total concentration and focus on the one and only true God Yeshua.

Each visit detailed a different holy experience, healing, transformation, and blessing. This was new and refreshing for me, as I watched in awe as the Spirit of God moved through the temple permeating each person present. The Scriptures came alive as Rabbi Gabriel spoke, bringing faith and hope to everyone. One week I would attend my congregation, the next week it would be the Mishkan David temple. However, most times I wanted to be at the Temple. Before long I became friends with the members, and I shared my daughter's battle with them. They told me not to worry and that they would be praying for her. Each week I visited, they asked about Juliette's progress. Can you imagine strangers praying and loving my daughter from a distance? How precious? In the movie "War Room" the actress portrays a woman who fought for her marriage, she cleared her closet, mind, and spirit through daily supplications to God, then she got the victory. A good friend asked me if I watched the movie. She did not know of my dire circumstances. I told her no, but that I would see it since she recommended it so highly to me. I got a chance to watch the movie and it was awe inspiring. It imprinted on my heart of how faith and trust in God can move mountains. I received more gusto to fight for my daughter from the clutches of the devil. Of course I did not empty my closet — it had too many clothes and shoes. I am ashamed to admit; but ladies, we know our short-comings as it relates to shopping. I separated the clothes until I found some space on the wall to write her name and what I was asking from God. I got a chair because I intended to stay on this subject with the Master until I got a result. I was determined and nothing was going to stop me. I told myself that she was dedicated to God, not the devil; Juliette was given to the Father from birth. After two weeks I was expecting a change, but nothing happened.

Early one afternoon while sitting in the living room with my mother, in walked a strange female with my daughter behind her. They both turned to walk away when I asked them to come in. The young woman was uncertain of what to do, so I beckoned her to come in again. She came in; I offered her a seat on the sofa. I saw that she was very uncomfortable, she glanced at me and it was not pleasing. There was a little anger in her facial expression. I tried to offer her something to drink; but she refused and they both left after Juliette got what they had come for. Later that day, my daughter apologized for breaking the agreement, because she had promised to respect my Christian principles. The more I prayed about the situation, the worse things seemed to be. I knew giving up meant defeat and destruction: I had to trust God in my dilemma. I told myself that there would be that silver lining and God would come through for me.

Months went by and I stayed in my closet praying. Every chance I got was devoted to the throne of grace and mercy. A few weeks passed and Juliette came home with a silver promise ring. She told me that she would be marrying this girl soon. I waited until her back was turned then I spoke in the wind of her presence, "That will never happen in the name of Jesus Christ of Nazareth, I rebuke it. You do not know the God I serve." I was not worried or afraid, but I knew prayer was the key. The more I fight, the more the devil pushes back. "This is my child," I said. "I gave her to God when she was born." It was important to remember that. One afternoon, she came and informed me that all her friends would be over for pizza and a movie. That evening my living room was filled with young people that I recognized from the previous churches I attended. This was not uncommon for me because my house was the place all the teenagers visited a lot for fun with my children. As I greeted everyone, I came upon an unfamiliar face which was not from any of the congregations I attended. It was the young woman I met in my living room a while back. I got upset because Juliette didn't tell me that the visit would have included her. I had never accepted their relationship. The more I thought about it, the angrier I got, but the Scriptures kept me grounded. "Be ye angry, and sin not, Let not the sun go down upon your wrath."

(Ephesians 4:26). I felt like she tricked me, and things couldn't have gotten worse because her friends were there. They accepted her lifestyle from the beginning, and to them, these Christian young adults, it was nothing that should bother me. That's the world we live in today. Being gay is common-place. I want to yell, scream, and have everyone leave my home.

My daughter could tell how upset I was, it showed on her face. I saw the concern and fear. She knew what she did was upsetting and wrong to me. I breathed deeply and walked back to my room with tears in my eyes. What just happened? I could not believe that the devil brought the fight to me in person, right there in my home. I went back to my room thinking about it for a while and then fell asleep. It was about 1:30 a.m. when I woke up again. Everyone was asleep except Juliette and a friend watching a movie in the living room. I walked back and heard snoring coming from her room. I mean, loud snoring. I called to Juliette to ask about the snoring noise that was coming from her room. She told me that it was her girlfriend. She had been born prematurely and her voice-box was not properly formed, so she has labored breathing while sleeping and spoke like a man with a deep, harsh tone. In that moment God did something to me. He placed a deep compassion in me, one that I never felt before. He impressed upon my spirit a love and sympathy that was unnatural. That feeling was not my own. Friends, I was overwhelmed with a compassion that enveloped my whole soul. God alone can give this feeling in such a time as this, but I walked away due to my selfish pride. I wanted to hold her and comfort her like my own child but I didn't.

This woman was in my daughter's room. How could I humanly be okay with that? She was my daughter's lover. This was unnatural, not Christian, and ungodly. Why was I feeling care and kindness towards her? Folks, when we seek God's intervention in anything, sometimes we do not like the answer He gives. He was working on my heart in the moment. We ourselves are lacking and He has to show us our heart too. In my imperfection I was asking for perfection. Nothing is wrong with that; however, I had to know that I was lacking in this situation too. Juliette's soul was not the only one in trouble: this woman was in the same battle and tribulation. Moreover, God loved her and died for her too. Through all my efforts trying to free my child from the grasp of evil, I never prayed for this woman, and to this day I still do not know her name.

We must strive to be like Christ. "Therefore if there is any encouragement in Christ, if there is any consolation of love, if there is any fellowship of the Spirit, if any affection and compassion, make my joy complete by being of the same mind, maintaining the same love, united in spirit, intended on one purpose. Do nothing from selfishness or empty conceit, but with humility of mind regard, one another as more important than yourselves" (Philippians 2:1-5). Don't merely look out for your own personal interests, but also for the interests of others. Have this attitude in yourselves, which is also in Christ Jesus. Where was the love I should have for this child? How selfish could I have been? Some Christian I proclaimed to be. "For the son of Man came to seek and save that which was lost" (Luke 19:10). Dear friend, do not despise each other—despise the sin. When our eyes are open to who God is, we become transformed by the renewing of our minds. "Therefore if anyone is in Christ, he is a new creature: old things are passed away: behold all things become new (2 Corinthians 5:17). I learned this lesson in a profound way my friends. As we press closer to God, He teaches our spirit His ways because "Our ways and thoughts are not His" (Isaiah 55:8). I thought about the Holy Spirit and how He impacted me so powerfully. I never told my daughter about what happened to me that night.

Following the incident, I had a dream. I dreamed that my daughter and her girlfriend were standing on a river bank and I was on the other side close to an open door behind me. To the left of me was a great rushing water coming toward us, but it was more directed to the both of them. It came and almost covered them, and in my spirit, I knew if the next flood of water came it would cover them and wash them away. The water was crystal clear. I could see right through to the bottom. In my spirit the Lord told me to go into the water and save both of them. I said to the lord, "I cannot swim. How can I do that?" I even reminded the Lord that Juliette is a fish; both my children swim very well. I asked why she cannot save herself and her partner. I am a non-swimmer. Why must I save them both? In my dream I yelled out to Juliette and told her to try and beat the next flood of water before it comes. The problem was that God became quiet, He stopped talking. She could not do what I asked because when I looked again, the water was almost upon them. I stepped out into the flood, grabbed both their arms together, and pulled them both to safety. I took them through the open door and we were all saved. Jesus is the open door (John 10:9). I didn't understand the dream until later. I tried to tell Juliette about it but she had nothing to say and showed no emotions. The Lord was telling me that they both needed saving, and I was to consider praying for both of them.

What a mighty God we serve! I continued going to the Mishkan David Temple. I was enjoying the worship and fellowship. One Friday night I sat alone speaking to God about my daughter and the situation of her sexual orientation. My lips were not moving and I was not verbalizing, but I was talking to God in my spirit. I was doing that for about ten minutes when out of nowhere I heard a voice. I opened my eyes and looked to see who was talking. A gentleman sitting two rows ahead of me said, "You know your daughter can change." I froze; I don't know why I still get startled when God shows me His miracles. I was praying to the Lord in my spirit, I was not expecting anyone to speak to me about my predicament, especially a man that I was not talking to. He then said, "See that lady over there? She was gay too and God healed her. Now she has a husband and daughter." I could not speak, because for one thing I felt invaded, and two, he was speaking my business to me, which I never shared with him. It never occurred to me that God was using him to communicate with me. As far as I was concerned, he was not even aware or knew of what he said to me. I told the man thanks, I was too shocked to ask him how he knew what I was praying about. The next thing I knew, the lady to whom the man referred came to me, and told me of her life transformation from lesbianism to a woman of faith. She showed me her past pictures wearing male garments, her tattoos, and her masculine hair-cut. I had to look twice to make sure it was her in the photos. Looking at her today, I give God thanks for his undying love and the price He paid (dying on the cross) to save us all. The young lady told me that she would help me pray for my daughter and one day she will worship here at the Mishkan David Temple too. I felt glad to know that the Lord is always there, and I was empowered to pray even more, as I was sure He was hearing my prayers. The Lord was showing me step by step that he was working his way to perfection in my daughter.

God went to the extent of showing His works through my church members from my previous congregation as well. The year was coming to a close, and it was time for the Women's Ministries secret sister banquet. Throughout the year of giving a gift to our secret sister, it was time for the revelation. All the ladies were excited to find out who their secret sister was. When my secret sister was revealed, I discovered she was an older widowed woman with not much to spare financially. I gladly received my gift, enjoyed the fellowship, and food, and went home. We had a wonderful time, I love the ladies, and they returned the love. When I got home and opened my package, it had hot dog baskets, another plastic gadget of some sort, and a very dusty old book. I placed everything aside and wiped off the book. It was written in 2005. She gave me what she could afford, and I appreciated it. The following day I passed the devotional (book) where I had placed it on the night stand, and the Spirit told me to pick it up and read it to the day and date. I did, and what I read was phenomenal. The page said, to your children, "first your son, the Lord is working his way through him; he is deeper than you think. To your daughter, respect her and her companion, do not show disgust, treat them well," I thought to myself what are the odds of a dusty old book revealing the truth of my two children, a boy and a girl, and speaking directly to who they were and what was going on in their lives.

I told my sister and friends about the book and what it said. It seemed that I was the only one impressed about this revelation. Yeshua is a personal God, when He speaks to your spirit only you can fully grasp the supernatural impact of it. God works in mysterious ways — His wonders to perform. I felt good in my spirit; something good was about to happen because God was sending so many messages to me. Not too long following that revelation, I got home a little tired and decided to go to bed early. I was falling asleep when in walked Juliette and she said, "Mom, I change my sexual orientation. I am no longer gay." Bless the Lord, oh my soul, the best news ever. If you had given me millions, it could not compensate for the joy of answered prayers. The she said, "Let's go to the Mishkan David, the temple where you have been going and experiencing worship, love, and fellowship." All this time she was listening to the experiences I had at the temple. Each night after the services, I would tell her stories of healing, sermons of revelation, and fellowshipping with the members. Many times I felt like I was talking to myself; but surely the experiences impacted her heart. The following Friday night we went to the temple, and she was well received by the members. Juliette fit in almost as if they knew her before. Everyone loved her and treated her like family; within three months of being there, she got engaged and was married. I have a wonderful son-in-law, Thomas. When I look at them, I see something that God Himself has joined together. It pleases my heart to know that Yeshua is in approval of their union. What God has joined together, let no man put asunder. Blessed be the name of the great I AM. Lastly, the ring came back in the mail, from the ungodly relationship. The young woman decided to return it and I happened to get it first. My mind went back to the day Juliette told me of her promise ring and I rebuked it. Out of respect I called my daughter and told her that the ring had come in the mail from her ex-girlfriend. She replied, "Mom, throw that into the garbage, please." I imagined that everything the devil sent to my daughter was garbage, in the hope to complete his distructive plan for her life. God gives good gifts, "every good and perfect gift comes from above" (John 1:17).

The Birth of My Son

Having children is a beautiful event. They are blessings from God. My son came four years after Juliette was born. During my first childbirth experience, everything was wonderful and I was pampered and well cared for. The birthing process was a different story. The pain was horrible and I labored for a long time even days. Several blood vessels in my eyes broke due to constant pushing. I ended up looking like something from a horror movie. My eyes were black and red for weeks, the doctor told me they would clear up and improve and they did.

Almost three years after the birth of our daughter, my husband and I decided to have another child. We tried on our own to get pregnant for nearly a year without success. This time we decided to seek a gynecologist who specialized in treating conditions of a woman's reproductive system to help in our situation. I was told that my hormone level was low and with treatment, things would improve. After three months of trying, I got frustrated and wanted to quit. The doctor asked me to try for one more month, which I did and I became pregnant. The feeling of accomplishment was great. Our daughter had asked us repeatedly to give her a companion. She claimed that we had each other and she had to play alone or be sent to the neighbors to play with their children. When our daughter received the good news, she was so happy that there would be another individual in the home and she would be the big sister.

In the back of my mind lurked the remembrance of labor pains. I did not want to feel that way again. I was happy and even elated to be having another child. I dearly love children. The more the merrier; but my husband felt differently. He had several children from his previous marriage, so two children were enough for this marriage. As things progressed, the doctor informed us that a cyst was also present in my womb the size of the growing embryo. He said that, unfortunately, one would grow larger than the other (the embryo or the cyst) and the smaller one will be pushed out. Simply explained, I could lose my son. My mind went back to how long and hard we tried to conceive and now this.

Well for some reason, I was not worried about the diagnosis but more worried about the pain. That told me everything would be okay, and sure thing Datta grew and the cyst diminished in size, never to return. I started talking to the Lord about my fears, the birth pains, and how worried I was about the ordeal to come. "For God did not give us a spirit of fear, but of power, love and a sound mind," (2 Timothy 1:7). When we read and study God's Word, we must not take them for granted; instead, we should believe them and feed on them. Develop a process of ingesting and living His Word into our daily life. "For the Word of God is alive and active, and sharper than a two-edged sword and piercing even to the dividing of soul and spirit, of both joints and marrow, and quick to discern the thoughts and intents of the heart." (Hebrews 4:12). Oh my God is great! Nothing is too hard for the Lord. Just believe in Him; He will help you to have faith, and His Holy Spirit will help your inward parts. This was what I told the Father. "Please Lord; I am anxious about the pain. Please take it away from me. I don't want to feel any pain because I remember how horrible the last birth was." When we believe that we are children of the Most High, we don't have to live like everyone else. Learn to claim the promises and use them to our benefit. I didn't realize that's what I was doing at the time. I felt like God is my father and asking Him to do things for me came naturally. I know how powerful He is and so nothing was exempt. I just expressed myself to the Lord. Every chance I got I talked to the Father about my feelings. After eight months, I went to look at my last sonogram and Datta was sucking his finger at times and appear to be drinking the amniotic fluid. The doctor told me this was the final time seeing him before his birth and gave me the next appointment to see him. In a few weeks, I went back and he told me all was well; but he was looking at me oddly. I asked him what was wrong. He asked me if I was feeling any pain and I replied no, and was shocked when the doctor enlightened me, that I was in full labor. He said each time I felt a tightening of the uterine muscle, which came briefly, it was contraction. I was in full blown labor without the labor pain. This was good. He did not understand what was happening so he told me to go to my mother's house, which I did.

As the day wore on into evening, I had fallen sleep. I woke up to feeling very uncomfortable. My water did not break but I was bleeding. I was not afraid. There was no pain. My mother was furious when she saw the situation. She asked how I could have done this to myself, and that I was in pain without telling anyone. There was no pain, she took me to the hospital and they rushed me in. I was not fully dilated so I had to wait. The bleeding was okay and there was no complication. The doctor came in and asked me if I was in pain and I told him I wasn't. I could tell that he did not believe me as he walked away looking strangely at me. Out came the nurse again, this time with a clipboard and some papers. She told me that it was time for my epidural. I asked her why and said it was routine because we signed for it at the beginning of the pregnancy. I was in no pain or distress, but to appease her I gave her the consent. Immediately following the procedure a rush of pain hit my body like a lightning bolt. It was so dreadful that I remembered my request to God. When things are worrisome and bad, we pray for help and God steps in, but as soon as things are better again, we forget. Worst of all, half of my body was enveloped in pain and the other half had no pain. That condition made me think that God was telling me something. First, He answers prayers; second, I must trust Him; and third never weaver in my belief. I knew better to please God not man. The lack of pain was unusual and strange. Yeshua came through for me. To honor God, I should have refused the epidural at all cost. That would have proven my faith to Him.

The decision was made by the doctor and the treatment team to give me another shot in order to have complete numbness and I refused. They claimed that the procedure was done incorrectly. I suffered pain which did not last too long; I had a lesson to learn. Indeed, this was a miracle. I treasure all my encounters with God and who He is to me. The Lord can be everything you need if you trust Him and have a relationship with Him. Find Him while there is still time. He is waiting for you to open your heart's door and let Him in. Regularly I tell my son about his birth and that he is a winner and survivor. I tell him how he conquered the syst and survived until birth. God wanted him to live. Children are precious and God has a plan for them. Our job is to guide them to the Lord through the Holy Spirit. As parents, if we don't trust in the Lord with all our hearts, mind, and spirit, we have absolutely nothing to leave our children. Solomon said it best when he declared that without God, everything else is vanity absolutely nothing.

The Holy Presence of God

The presence of God is a holy and wonderful experience. I knew He was with me, and He manifests Himself to me when I call upon Him. The women of the church I attended went to a women's ministry retreat like clock-work every year. I was not particularly interested in that area of ministry. However, the ladies were all excited to go on this retreat. When they returned, a report was given to the church of all their spiritual experiences. Somehow, I never felt moved or inspired to attend. One day the church clerk came to me and asked why I never went with the ladies. My response was that I never felt the need to and I was okay with that. She went on to say that once I experience it, I would go every year. I attended the next women's ministry retreat. It was wonderful, just getting away from the responsibilities of home and focusing on God was the best. I love my family and my home; but this time someone else was making my breakfast for the next three days and I didn't have to worry about cleaning or taking care of the children.

The services were educational and the facilitators were all professionals. We shopped at the nearby stores that had sales, and we purchased Christian books from the booths prepared at the retreat. The best part of it was being there among thousands of women worshipping and praising Yeshua in one accord, it was amazing. I went every year after that and it became routine. I knew what to expect from the seminars. They had eloquent speakers demonstrating no spirituality, the banquet, shopping, delicious food, thank you and goodbye...see you next year.

This particular year I attended the retreat and it was not quite the same. Something spiritual happened to me. Months ahead of attending, the Holy Spirit told me to get an anointing, which I shared with no one. I felt like the folks in my congregation were not spiritual enough to do it. My church at that time had so many discords and confusion that ran from leadership down to the regular members. I developed a rebellious spirit and mostly kept everything I was feeling inside. When I got to the retreat nothing changed; however, I got some time to myself. From nowhere came this lady and she said to me, "I can anoint you." I got upset and asked her why. I had not said anything about what the Holy Spirit told me months before, so I walked away. The following day it was time for the seminars, I decided to attend only one and it was about prayer. Usually there were five or six meetings going on simultaneously, and we could switch between them every twenty minutes. I felt like one would be enough, so I went to the very last one.

I sat by the door in case it became boring or I got disinterested I could simply leave quietly. As I entered the room, it was packed with little to no space, and the speaker asked her assistant to close the doors for less interruption. There went my plan. The session was interactive. We were asked to stand and move forward, closer to the stage. The speaker introduced herself and began expounding about praying and different prayers. She said, "When you pray hold your hand to the heavens, it makes a difference." She said to express yourself and talk to God as if He is physically in front of you, and not to be afraid to address Him because He loves you and He is open to hearing your prayers. For the first time I was curious and I felt empowered to do just what she said. We all held our hand high and started praying when suddenly the entire room became pitch black. There was a big bright chandelier in the middle of the ceiling. I closed my eyes expecting the light to still reflect through my eyelids. But, there was no light, just thick darkness, so I opened my eyes to see if I was blind or not. I could see, thank God. For the rest of the session, I was scared so I kept my eyes open until the end. I questioned what it was and the meaning, it was a strange happening. When the twenty minutes were up, I went to the facilitator and shared my experience. She told me that I was spiritually sensitive and what happened was supernatural. I wanted full clarity, I wished she explained more. I questioned why I went in the first place and thought my plan had backfired. Upon leaving the seminar I met up with my roommate in the reception area of the hotel. I informed her of my experience and she told me to ask God about it. The woman who offered to anoint me was heading in our direction, this time she offered to anoint me and I accepted. My roommate joined us, we were taken to her room and we all knelt. The lady poured the oil on my forehead and I closed my eyes to pray when the entire room went pitch black again, no light was coming through. My goodness, that was scary. I opened my eyes again and decided to remain visually aware. When the prayer was done, I kept the occurrence to myself for the rest of the retreat. The thick darkness occupied my mind and enveloped my whole being.

Dear friends Jesus said, "For I am the Lord your God who takes hold of your right hand, and says to you, do not fear I will help you" (Isaiah 41:13). Keep this text in your heart when the spirit of fear comes, it will leave. The best way to tackle any problem is to ask God's help by telling Him about it. My reason for being profound and fearful was the thought that darkness was never good. One should walk in the light (John1:6). Heaven is light, hell is darkness, so this experience created a sense of destruction and doom and no clear meaning was coming through to me. On my way home on the bus, the ladies were singing beautiful hymns, but I was quiet, I never felt like joining them. My mind was occupied with the dark episode. When I got home, I did not share the incident with my family. A couple of days following my return, I decided to tell God and ask Him for clarity. Within the same week of praying, God gave me a vision. I was standing in a large room without a roof looking straight into the blue sky. I had some Christian literature for distribution in my hand. This activity is something I've enjoyed doing from an early age, distributing tracks and telling people about Jesus Christ. Somehow, this time the brochures were blown and scattered all about, and I could not catch or gather them by myself. I tried to but soon I needed some help. Out of nowhere came this beautiful causation girl with blue eyes like the sea. She started helping me to pick up the brochures and we were making progress. I used my foot to stop one of the sheets when a voice from heaven said: "Don't put your foot on the Word." I felt reprimanded so I hurriedly stopped. After picking up all the pamphlets, she went into a room like a restroom and closed the door, and just like that she was gone. I wanted to thank her for helping me so I ran after her and knocked on the door. She did not open it, but she quoted Exodus 20 and I woke up.

I allowed a day to pass before delving into the Scriptures because I was unsure of what awaited me in them. Now, she did not give me a specific verse so I knew that I must read the full chapter. I found a quiet place and started reading Exodus 20 in its entirety. The Ten Commandments are in that chapter, and in verse 20 it states that Moses told the people not to fear for God has come to prove them and that His fear may be before their faces that they sin not, this fear is love. Then verse 21 states: "And the people stood afar off and Moses drew near unto the thick darkness where God was". I got it, God was with us praying. We were in the presence of the Almighty. It was a mind-blowing revelation. Only Jehovah can do that. He was with everyone present praying but He revealed himself to me in my shallow, rebellious state. God knew that I was drifting away from Him because of what was happening in the church at that time, and He wanted me back. I could not understand and became fearful because of the distance I placed between myself and God. I should have separated myself from everything and focused solely on Him through the rough patch. God knows us more than we know ourselves. He can give us exactly what is needed to fix our problem. Christian friends, don't be afraid of anything verse 20 tells us, "For God is come to prove us, and that his fear may be before our faces that we sin not." What a reassurance. I went to the session expecting nothing and received everything. "You have seen that I have talked with you from Heaven" He spoke to the Israelites but He also spoke to me from heaven when He told me not to put my foot on the Word. I will continue telling others of the Word. We serve a true and living God. My hope is built on nothing less than Jesus's blood and righteousness. "Hear O Israel: The Lord our God is one. Love the Lord your God with all your heart and with all your soul and with all your strength" (Deuteronomy 6:4-5). Love the Lord with your everything and do not be afraid to trust Him with your life.

The Book – A Principle of Faith

I like to read mostly spiritual books, especially the Bible. I love to find the Holy Spirit's messages between the pages. When the revelation comes, I get a spiritual high. Nothing is more enlightening than understanding and receiving God's Words. The more I read, the more I am in awe of who God is and how much I need Him. One can never get enough. There is always more. The Father is endless, His bounties extend far more than we can ever imagine or comprehend. Reading the Bible brings me to new experiences in Christ each time. I was sitting at home one morning just thinking of spiritual books written that I would love to read but could not afford them. The prices of these books range from sixty to one-hundred and fifty dollars. I believe the Word of God should be affordable. God paid the price already when He died on the cross. What good is the Word is you cannot afford it financially?

Coming from a religious background, there were several authors I admired and wanted to purchase their writing, which was out of my financial reach, so of course I decided to ask the Lord. My first thought when seeking a good spiritual book to read was to ask Yeshua to choose for me. I told Him that I wanted one that would help me spiritually. One that was inexpensive and well written. I told Him that I was going to the thrift shop to look for that book and He should show it to me.

I love going to the thrift shop because of the vintage things I find there. The old antiques tell a story and I enjoy the histories. I drove to the store and went straight towards the library of books. As I was looking through the rows, I saw a book I knew. My father had one but I never read it. He was an avid reader of the Bible and religious books; this particular book was big, brand new and paperback. Instantaneously I knew this was the book. If I should purchase this copy in a regular book store, it would cost at least forty-five to sixty dollars. The name of the book is the *Desire of Ages*. It was like new and beautiful. I looked at the price which was written in green marker. It was two dollars and ninety-nine cents. I paid for it immediately it was so heavy, shiny and clean like new. Thank you God I prayed silently, for answering my prayers. I took the book home and could not believe my good fortune. In this case, I was specific with God again. I explained what I was looking for. He granted my wish with a price even lower than my expectations. This was fantastic! I told Yeshua that I wanted a book which would help me spiritually, teaching me His Words and would give me knowledge and understanding as I read. He came through for me glory to His name.

In crept another thought: What if there were more books? Remember I asked God for a book; but in my curiosity and greed, I went back to the store and looked again. Before I started looking through the rows I saw the same book, the same name, only this time it was compact in smaller print. I felt so embarrassed and overcome with guilt and shame. Yes I had two books, but what does my action denote? God heard my request and granted me precisely what I asked, in His divine kindness and wisdom. My job was to accept His gracious love and give praise and worship. I listened to that other voice which told me to look for other books. God could have turned His back on me causing me to lose everything. Instead, He forgave me and in His mercy He placed the same book there saying, "My child this is what you asked of me, Trust me." I got the message right away and gave the second book to my daughter. She took the book but could not appreciate the gift at that time. The lesson was mine and thank God I understood.

Many times the Lord gives us good gifts that we trade for a lie. The devil comes and steals it away, leaving us broken and lost. "We must put on the whole armor of God that ye may be able to stand against the wiles of the devil."(Ephesians 6:11). This book was meant to enlighten me, and the devil knew what I asked of God so he intercepted, hoping to derail the plan. In every step of our lives, we must put Christ first. "The Lord is our keeper; the Lord is the shade at your right hand" (Psalm 121:5).

Lastly, ask of the Lord. He is the giver of good gifts. "As sinful individuals we give good gifts to our children, how much more shall our heavenly Father give good things to them that asked of Him". (Matthew 7:11). We give each other, including our children, worldly things to make them happy. These things have no substance, they rot and fade away. It is time to tell our loved ones about the gospel. How Christ died on the cross to save us. Let's give them the Word and teach it to our children while giving God thanks for everything.

The Death of My Father

This part of my writing is the hardest. The memories of my father's passing are as plain as yesterday. The rest of my siblings were hurting tremendously, as well as our mother. The migration to America came in stages. My younger sister and brother went with my parents first. Three years following their departure, another younger brother and I finally joined them, and later two other siblings followed. When I saw my father again for the first time, he looked well. We lived in a fine looking home and started adjusting to a new life in a different world. Being together with the family once again was delightful.

My father went fishing on the pier every Sunday, much to my delight. In Florida, the waterways are breathtakingly beautiful. The big ships, boats, and jet skis are a few of the sightseeing attractions free of cost. Sometimes on Sunday night, we would go bowling. My sister met her husband on one of those trips. My parents loved bowling, especially my mother but slowly Dad refrained from that sport. I noticed that his relationship with the church was just as vibrant as it was at home in Jamaica and he was beloved by everyone. I was told that upon Dad's arrival in the US, he went straight from the plane to the hospital. That's when he got the diagnosis, kidney failure, and dialysis was the next course of action. Over the years this procedure took a toll on him, and before long he became weaker and less active. This was why he stopped bowling. Soon after, he started forgetting things, and other cognitive issues followed. The led, acid, and asbestos were tools of his trade. He made from scratch without the proper protection, which compromised his health in a deadly way.

He had brain surgery following a CAT scan that showed a large mass on the brain. It was not malignant. After the surgery, he had to take medication for the seizures. Seeing my father in the hospital was painful. He was a body builder, very active, and health conscious. There is a saying that what you do not know won't hurt you. This statement is not true, for the lack of education in the craft of his trade; my Dad paid the ultimate price. Later when he came home from the hospital, my mother was having difficulty caring for him at home. She worked nights and he needed round-the –clock assistance so she decided the best place for Dad was a nursing home. I did not like this decision, but it was necessary for his proper care and treatment. The family visited him a lot, but on one of my visits, he had stopped communicating altogether. The nurses told me how delightful Dad was and that he never complained about anything. I wished I had more time with my father. His knowledge of people and their behaviors was unprecedented. It didn't matter who the individual was, he could reach them with love and understanding. He was a people person, very kind and respectful. My father gave and never asked in return. Truly he was a man of God.

One Tuesday morning I woke up in tears from a dream I had. I dreamed that my father succumbed to his illness and died. That day at work I hid in my office and cried. I called my mother and told her and she accepted the message. In the dream, I saw my father in his illness giving specific instructions to one of my older brothers. He said as soon as he dies and is buried, my brother should open the grave and connect him to the tubes (life support), which will keep him alive.

There was also a woman present, one of our church members, saying he was not dead. She was in the church at his funeral claiming he was alive. In the dream, I was annoyed at her because he had passed away and was placed in a morgue before burial; but she insisted it was a trick and he was pretending to be dead. There was one thing I saw that I didn't understand and it bothered me even after I woke up. My father's coffin was in the mouth of a crane. I had no clue of its meaning. There were other things in my dream that I have forgotten; but these things I mention are still clear to me. Three weeks after the dream, we got the news that Dad had fallen and was placed in the hospital. When I got there, I saw the woman in my dream who had questioned my father's death. I was surprised because she attended the same church I did; but I was unaware of her profession. She was a nurse and she worked at the hospital where my father was admitted. Her personality was pleasing; she took good care of Dad knowing we are all of the family of God.

The doctors informed us that Dad's organs were shutting down and he was going through a process called weeping. After a few more days, the doctor told us to make a decision to take him off the breathing tube (life support) and at that time he would pass. Looking back at my dream, this was God's way of helping me through the process. He knew how much I adored my father and the pain of watching him die would be very hard and difficult. Things he said in the dream caused me to believe my father wanted to live. The doctors explained that this was the best course of action because all his organs were already gone. The only thing keeping him alive was the breathing tube. That's exactly what my Dad told my brother in my dream. Taking him off life support was the hardest decision of our lives. We all agreed except the sibling Dad told to reconnect him as soon as he was buried. I did not share this vision with my brother as it was too painful for me to repeat. My brother cried so much, he refused to agree, so we went ahead and my father passed.

The funeral was sad and somber. My mother remained strong. We followed behind the hearse to the burial plot. I looked up with tears in my eyes and there it was — the coffin in the crane just like my dream. My mother is extremely secretive and did not tell anyone in the family that Dad was being placed in a tomb. I looked in amazement as the crane picked up the coffin and placed it in vault. The part of the dream that eluded me the whole time was finally explained and revealed.

The Lord is my comforter; He knew what was coming so He softened the blow by telling me ahead of time. "Blessed be the God and Father of our Lord Jesus Christ, the Father of mercies and God of all comfort, who comforts us in our entire affliction, so that we may be able to comfort those who are in any affliction, by the comfort with which we ourselves are comforted by God" (2 Corinthians 1:3-5).

Months passed and I had another dream. This time I saw my Dad as I never saw him before. He was about twenty-five-years old, quite young and handsome. He was wearing a well-tailored brown suit, black shiny shoes, and looked like a gentleman. He passed by slowly looking at me without talking; but I knew what he said. He had to go somewhere that I could not go. He had to speak to someone before he could speak to me again. He was so peaceful and changed in a newness of life. In the dream, I felt disappointed because he did not spend time with me and then he was gone. I totally forgot the dream until a few days after when I got a call from my sister. She was excited. She said "I saw Dad and he looked young." Before she could go further, I stopped her and said, "Let me describe him for you," I gave her detail upon detail of how he looked in my dream and described his attire. The phone went silent. After a while she started speaking again. She asked me how I knew, and I told her I had the same dream.

We read in 1 Thessalonians 4:13, "Brothers and sisters, we do not want you to be uninformed about those who sleep in death so that you do not grieve like the rest of mankind, who have no hope." God is so good; his promises are sure, be blessed.

An Ill-Fated Flight

Visiting my homeland brings back so many childhood memories. I get to see my family and spend some time basking in the beauty of the island. I never get tired of returning to the place of my birth. One of the beautiful sights I love are the mountains and hills in the background that appear when arriving to the island. Upon landing, the scene is picturesque with lush green vegetation, colorful houses on the hillsides, and the inviting view of the beaches, which provide calm and peace for the spirit. In the summer of 2011, I went to see my family and friends, and we had a fabulous time together. The flight to Jamaica was fine and before long I was at my aunt Glentine's home. I was not alone, my fiancé and I decided to visit our families separately. I went into the city where my aunt lived, and he went to the rural areas of the Island. The plan was to meet again in the city following our visit with our respective families and fly back to Florida.

I slept a lot due to the lazy hot summer. I was on my mini vacation and relaxation was my main goal. The week went by too fast; it was time to return home. At the airport, we got ready for boarding and got on the plane. My fiancé was sitting in the middle row, and I was sitting in the aisle. I had just secured myself with the seatbelt when in my spirit I heard "ill-fated flight". My whole body quaked because I knew what it meant; moreover, I knew what I heard. There was no doubt about the information I had just received. In my mind I thought of telling my companion; but I did not want to alarm him. This was a spiritual thing and others might have a different view on this kind of message. As I sat there, I prayed to God asking Him for help to move forward. More than ten minutes passed, and I was frozen in fear and questioning. I thought of going to the flight attendant and asking for assistance to get off the plane; but the door was already shut. And what about the other passengers? Then I wanted to inform the pilot that the plane was going to crash if we tried to leave. If I did that for sure I would be escorted off the plane with a call to the Fort Lauderdale airport that a passenger was taken off the plane due to endangerment to self and other passengers. I would be labeled as being crazy or mentally ill, so I remained quiet while still praying to God for assistance in the matter. Later I remember telling my younger brother Paul about the event. He responded by saying that under no circumstances would he have remained on the plane.

More than thirty minutes had passed since I received the alert. Yeshua warned me for a reason, I was thankful that He did. The problem was evident, I froze in fear too scared to act. Suddenly, the pilot spoke over the intercom and said, "This is your pilot speaking. We are having some difficulty and our engineers are working on the problem. The weather is great and we will be leaving in another fifteen minutes." The lump in my throat subsided. God heard my desperate plea for help. Even though he told me in advance, I could not help myself because of what I thought people might think or say. God must take center stage in our lives; as long as we live in the light of the Father, nothing others say or do to us should hold us back. We are hopeless without the Messiah. He is the only one that can save us. "Believe in the Lord Jesus Christ and ye shall be saved"(Acts 16:31). I was calm and feeling a bit better; but the trouble was not over. More than fifteen minutes had gone by and I was still on the plane. The pilot spoke again, this time he asked for more time. Everyone sat patiently hoping to get to Florida soon.

I can imagine there were individuals that were flying for the first time, little children and others anxiously waiting to reach their destination. After waiting for what seemed like a lifetime, the pilot finally said, "This is your pilot speaking; unfortunately, we are unable to leave at this time. We must disembark." Everyone had to get off the plane. I watched out the window as the plane was driven like a bus to the terminal and everyone evacuated. This was the one time in my life when I knew for sure (and seeing with my two eyes) that God saved me. To Yeshua be all the glory. Great things He has done. When the passengers got off the plane, they were cursing foul languages and arguing. Some were complaining and threatening to report the pilot and the airline.

God had saved them from a sure and horrible death. The cross comes to mind. How wickedly Jesus was crucified and died to save our lives while the crowd cried to crucify Him. Jesus in his tender mercy asked the "Father to forgive them for they knew not what they do" (Luke 23:34). This time I knew better so I sang praises to the Lord for his mercies ever so true. My rejoicing will last for a lifetime. I will worship and praise the holy name of Yeshua forever. Later that evening, we boarded another flight. I was not afraid, and the flight back home was fine. In my bed that night, I had many thoughts. One of them was that God didn't have to tell me anything. This event could have transpired with the pilot's announcements and the passengers, including me, getting off the plane; or it could have simply crashed and everyone died. God must have a plan for my life, and the other passengers as well. What was mine? Today I try to live my life in a holy place so that God can use me. "I delight to do thy will Oh my God; yea thy law is written in my heart"(Psalm 40:8).

The Deceptive Engagement

"God is our refuge and strength, a very present help in trouble" (Psalm 46:2). We have a tendency to see only what is immediately in front of us without seeing the big picture. Often times, we do what pleases us, without seeking God's advice before acting. When the ramifications beset us, we call on Him to clean up the mess. After my divorce, I met a gentleman in college and we became very good friends. He introduced me to his wife, and the friendship has lasted until today. He knew that I believe in Jesus. He is Jewish of the orthodox faith; but we never allowed our differences to come between our friendship. I completed the master's program in criminal justice and moved on to work at a mental health center's forensic department. He had a few more classes to complete the program, so after a few months we ended up working at the same company. It was a surprise for both of us to work together, and the relationship grew. I went to his home on a few occasions for dinner, and one evening he told me of an associate he knew. He said this man was a decent fellow and he started playing matchmaker. Deep down I knew that I was not ready for dating or to be in a relationship because my divorce was still looming and the infidelity was still fresh in my mind. I was not ready to trust anyone just yet.

I was living at my mother's house with my two children. The courts ordered the house I lived in with my ex-husband to be sold and shared between both parties, which I refused and allowed him to keep. There were too many bad memories and I wanted to be done with it all. Months passed and my schoolmate never spoke of him again. One day I got a call from a man who introduced himself and told me that he heard many good things about me. He mentioned my friend's name from college and proceeded to ask me out for dinner. I told him that I was not interested in dating anyone just yet and thanked him for calling. Six months later, he called again. My mother insisted that I go on a date with him and not push him away like the last time. I finally gave in and we went out to dinner. He was charming, caring, and personable. We discussed my faith and I introduced him to God and my church friends. We dated for a while and I felt more comfortable with him.

This man was dutiful and assisted me with all my programs in the women's ministries department where I was the ministry leader. He was very clean, well-kept and polite. I never wanted for anything, and his support was wonderful. The church community admired him because of his dedication. We dated for more than a year; and other couples who met after us got married. I was not really interested in moving forward just yet and avoided the subject. Two other couples who came to our congregation and were married and that's when the pressure from the church mounted. He eventually got baptized and started coming to church more regularly. One day, I received a call from one of my church elders, who told me that he had my best interest at heart. He told me that it was time to make the decision to marry. The elder informed me that my friend was baptized now, and we had been dating for a long time. Another elder called and said I should not marry anyone until I was ready. No one should make that decision for me, and he was right.

I believe the church has enough important issues to take into consideration other than my singleness. I felt a little betrayed knowing that they we talking about me in meetings and sent their generals to complete the task. Because of this, my friend and I started discussing engagement just to appease my church. Imagine that! The church happiness came before mine. Finally we got engaged, what followed that was a sick feeling. Yes, he was great but something was very wrong and I felt it strongly. We did not set a date; but the ring spoke volumes to the onlookers and the immediate pressure was off. As the months passed, the feeling lingered. My attraction to him was never overwhelming from the beginning; but, he grew on me and I was overcome with his dedication and attention.

God is first place in my life; but I never went to Him in the beginning of this relationship to discuss this person or ask Him what he thought. Looking back, I did the same thing with my previous husband. He was handsome, charming, and dedicated. It was hard not to fall for him when he pursued me. I brought him into the church, he got baptized, and we became married. Marriage is of God. He merges the heart. We must not treat it lightly. In the beginning, God created marriage. He made a couple — male and female. He brought them together Himself (Genesis 2:18). Christians must follow Christ's example. We do not know how to decide or who is right for us. Ask Him to choose for you. I realized that I had made the same mistake. This meant that the first lesson was not learned, and it was being repeated. Months passed and I never got over the overwhelming feeling of emptiness. I felt as if there was no substance in this portentous union.

This is the time to ask for help, so I called upon God for help. I asked Him to show me what I was sensing. I prayed earnestly about it and left it alone. Time went by and I completely forget about the prayer. One day following church services, I was feeling so happy and blessed. We had communion and we went home with family for lunch. I just walked in the door when my phone rang. I decided not to answer it because I wanted to stay in the presence of the Lord and the peace that He gave me that day. The phone kept ringing, so I finally answered it and the voice on the other end said, "My husband is paying your phone bill". Well, for a moment I thought she had the wrong number. My answer was that I was presently engaged and gave her the name of my fiancé. She started crying. The lady told me that he was her husband for many years. She got my number from a receipt which fell from his pocket on the bathroom floor and she found it. I was shocked and in disbelief; but I kept calm and in control. After we spoke for a few minutes, she explained that her relationship with him was from their teenage years. They were not married; but in a common law union where they were living together with two children.

As it turned out this lady was a sweet person. She was devastated and felt cheated because he was getting ready to marry another woman. I told her that we would talk later and I hung up the phone. My mind went into reverse. I recalled my worrisome feeling about this whole relationship, my previous marriage, and what I had asked God about. The answer came a week following my request to Him. God is such a wonderful savior; He will protect you at all costs. He said ask, seek, knock — His range is not limited. God will answer you — just trust Him, we are His beloved children. He died on the cross to save us, and nothing is too hard for the Lord. He answered my prayer and saved me from my mess.

Following the news, I called my fiancé and he came running. I asked him about his common law wife and children, which he denied. He claimed someone was trying to wreck our relationship. After explaining what I knew, including his young children, a boy and a girl, he could not deny the facts further. He gathered his jacket in embarrassment and left. The heavy feeling left immediately. I felt free and emancipated. When my children heard what happened, my daughter took it badly. We held each other in disbelief. My friends and family were shocked; they loved him, and felt sure he was the right person for me. Weeks following my revelation, I dreamed that I saw him in a food chain store where we shopped together frequently, so I avoided that one. I decided to visit the same store in a different location. I was with a friend in the store when she told me not to turn around. We were standing in the check-out line. She said it was my fiancé, but I could not help myself. I turned around. He was in line with his partner. He almost died of fright; his eyes begged me not to say anything, which I wouldn't. God physically proved to me that he was with someone else by showing me the both of them together. I switched stores but could not run away from God's revelation.

Thank Yeshua for His precious blood and how He can love me completely, when none other can. God alone knows everything. Never trust in what doesn't seem right. "Trust in the Lord with all your heart and lean not unto your own understanding but in all your ways acknowledge him and he will direct your paths" (Proverb 3:5).

Home

Where is home? Some people say it's where the heart is and that contentment anywhere can prove to be home. I know that my ultimate home is God's promise in John 14:2-3 which states, "In my Father's house are many mansions, If it were not so I would have told you. I go to prepare a place for you and if I go and prepare a place for you I will come again, and receive you unto myself, that where I am there ye may be also". I am longing to go home because my kingdom is not of this world. My Father, who is in heaven, is waiting to welcome me. He wants me to enter into the joy of my Lord (Matthew 25:21). I had the pleasure of working with some beautiful children from a program called the Little Lamb ministries. It is geared toward young children with parents in prison and who need help physically and spiritually. I received a call from a conference representative from the church I attended. She explained the circumstances of the children and the dire needs they had. I asked her how she got my information because the church has many different ministries; but she chose mine. She told me a member gave my information to her and so she called.

I went to see the children; their ages ranged from seven months to eight years of age. There were four of them, two girls and two boys. These children were beautiful, loving, and longed for care. They lived with their grandmother who was the mainstay. She also had two older twin boys, maybe eleven or twelve years old, and they all lived together in a rental home. The house was untidy, disorganized, and in need of structure. The children had no food, the cupboards were empty. They slept on mattresses on the floor, and the younger children needed proper grooming. The following week in church, I called a meeting to address the issues presented of the children in need. The response was great. The women got in gear, they purchased pretty dresses and suits of various sizes, others brought bows for their hair, and a special friend went with me to purchase shoes for them. After a while the trunk of my car was filled with supplies for the children. I got diapers, toiletries, bedding, and hygiene products. Members asked to donate money, because they were too busy to go out and purchase things for them. I spoke with the treasurer and she opened an auxiliary account, which was used to assist the family members, to cut the boys' hair and other immediate financial needs.

At that time I was going through some special issues of my own. I was renting and living on the water-front of a preserve. It was beautiful, each morning I woke up to nature with its wonderful green bounty of the different plants and flowers. My son went fishing every evening after school; he loved fishing like my father. Bird watching was a thing I did because they were right there for the viewing. The birds had so many different sounds and their plumage resembled the rainbow. God is amazing, He is found in everything He created. I loved living there, but it was time to leave. The rental company decided to upgrade, and as they did the price also increased. I could not afford to live in my paradise anymore, so I got a realtor to assist me in finding a decent place within my budget to live. I wanted to purchase a home but I planned on doing that a bit later.

I was at work one afternoon when the phone rang; it was my realtor, a Godly man. He told me there was a problem. He said my record showed that I was evicted before and this situation caused hindrances in finding rentals. I was surprised because I was never evicted, disposed, or asked to leave before. The problem was that my records showed differently. I asked my realtor to give me the address of the eviction; when he did, I started laughing. The address he gave me was the place I was presently living, he laughed too and thought it was strange. He was puzzled and did not know what was happening, but I did. The devil was backing me into a corner hoping that I would focus on myself. If he can place my attention on problems, then I would give little or no attention to the children. There was a catch however, I had to leave within the month and the pressure was on to find another place while having such a compromising problem. The leasing office was told in advance that I would not be signing another year's lease.

The situation intensified when I could not move due to the flaw placed on my record. The leasing company was willing to give me a letter stating that this was a flaw from the recent owners. They said it would take months to properly clear that situation from my record. I was so stressed and frustrated to tears. I prayed to God to come to my rescue again. During this time the family of the children contacted me about bedroom furniture for two of the small children. I went back to the church and told them of the added need. Right after the divine service, I was promised a bedroom set, dining set, and a living room furniture set. The ladies and I arranged for transportation, two deacons answered the call. Before delivery we had to clean up and organize the rooms. The next step was to schedule the date and time to get the job done.

I was standing by the church entrance when a member who looked like Moses (for lack of a more accurate description), approached me with his wife. I had seen them in church on a regular basis. They were quiet, well-respected members with whom I had little affiliation. He said to me, "Sister Tedim, I wished you had informed me of the need for furniture in the past. In my job we have to donate unwanted furniture when repairing homes." I told him that I was unaware of his profession but since he was in the field, could he also keep his eyes open for rentals for me? He looked me in the eyes and said "You want somewhere to live? I answered "yes" then he said "I want you to go into the community or city of your choosing, and find a place for one hundred and fifty thousand dollars. I will purchase it for you to live in. Then you can pay me whatever rent you can afford." It does not get any better than that with Jesus Christ. In that moment it was the best thing that could have happen to me. My God has cattles on a thousand hills. This is my Father's world. Why should my heart be sad? Where I had nothing, now I could choose. I looked at his wife and laughed in disbelief. The story of Sarah in the Bible came to mind, she laughed too when she was told of her upcoming miracle. I honestly thought he was joking so I said to his wife, "Your husband likes to be funny?" Her reply was that he was dead serious, and I should start looking right away. My cares went away, I knew it was done; God took my heavy burden away. Just like that it was gone.

The realtor and I had three weeks to find a home. Sounds impossible? Nothing is impossible with God. "He is the Alpha and the Omega" (Revelation 22:13). That Sunday, the deacons delivered the furniture for the children, and during the week we gave them provisions from the food bank. A sister and I went back to have worship with them. The home looked better and the children started recognizing the church members when they visited their home. I took them to church on several occasions and the members were very happy to see them. They received lots of hugs and kisses, with tender loving care. What was most important was that the children experienced God's love in action, through the members' abundant support.

As the time grew closer to leave the rental facility, we had a few failed attempts fortunately, we were able to find a home suited for me to move, and in the right time. The town home was spacious and comfortable. It was a three bedroom, just enough for my children and I. The realtor and I knew it would take a miracle to get the paperwork completed in such a short time. I told the realtor not to worry it would be okay because God was the author of the whole thing. Another surprise came when my realtor knew the selling agent. They were able to complete the closing process without a hitch. When God is working for you, there are no complications, just results. Bless the name Yeshua.

Days before leaving I heard a voice clearly say, "Matthew 10:12". I jumped up immediately and grabbed my Bible. I did not want to forget the verse. I opened it quickly and it said, "And when you get into the house, salute it." When I read it, my heart was lifted. God was not finished with me just yet. I was not too sure of what it meant, but I had an idea. That day I called the realtor, who was also an elder from my church, and I asked him to come with me along with a few deaconesses to pray at my new home. They came, we worshipped and gave God thanks for His blessings. There were six of us, this was my way of saluting the home and obeying Gods wishes.

The Bible says faith as small as a mustard seed brings results (Luke 17:6). I know to Whom I should run for my sustenance, so I stay grafted in the vine. He never leaves me or forsakes me. Just do as Jesus says and love Him first with all your heart. "If you love me keep my commandments" (John 14:15). I continued to work with the children until their mother was released from prison. The church was happy to assist her financially through the auxiliary fund provided. On two occasions we were able to give her money from the balance. She took the role of mother for the children, and the family was invited to the church, including the father. They all came, and we hoped to have continued attendance from them. Their visits were short lived as they moved away. I saw them a few times in the community but they never engaged. The last time I saw them we hugged, and I was so happy to see the children laughing and playing. Their situation must have changed for the better.

When working for the Lord, we must do whatever we can for as long as possible. There is always something to do in the vineyard. The harvest is ripe, the end is near, tell a friend about God. Testify of Yeshua's miracles in your life and lead souls to Christ. One day the Lord will say "well done my child". And the King shall answer and say unto them, "Verily I say unto you, inasmuch as ye have done it unto one of the least of these my brethren, ye have done it unto me." (Matthew 25:40).

The Trip to Israel

Israel is an amazing place to visit. For years I have been told of its wonders and beauty by the members of the Mishkan David temple and other individuals who have been there before. For three years, I have been attending the temple, I've dreamed of going but my finances would not allow it. When people I know returned from visiting Israel, they championed its beauty and spiritual awareness. The place is just awesome. They claimed that one must visit for oneself to have an experience because words cannot express its wonders. In my imagination, I saw the garden tomb where Jesus was laid, the Jordan River, and the Sea of Galilee. I was besieged with a longing to be there.

After services I was in a group of ladies who were getting ready to leave for home. One of them told the group that she was going to Israel that year. I made mention that I wanted to go too. Someone said "If you want to go God will make a way". This happened around the time my daughter had her life-changing experience and started attending the temple. That night my daughter declared that she was going. Now we had a joint venture. I love to travel, and Juliette was excited about visiting Israel just like I was. We started saving and putting money away for the trip, and in no time we both had the deposit. As the months passed, we became more and more excited and then something bad happened. My mother hit her head against the wall in her bedroom and she was taken to the hospital. She stayed there for more than a week, and the doctors decided to send her to a rehab facility due to her weakened state. Mom had lost too much weight and the doctors wanted her to get stronger by exercising and eating normally before going back home. Prior to the accident, Mom knew I was planning to go to Israel; but now she became indifferent to the idea of me leaving. In the nursing facility, the nurses informed me that she might not be able to remain there as she was disturbing the other patients and being difficult. When they showed me some of the damages Mom did, I could not accept or believe it. Mom was not violent. She gets angry but not physical, especially in her older years. My sister and I begged her to behave or else they would discharge her to other, more restrictive facilities. As the time drew closer to the date of our trip Mom became different. She stopped communicating with me. Sometimes she was angry and distrustful of me and almost acted as if she did not want to see me. Friends went to visit and she would be receptive and engaging with them; but when they left she would shut down again. I continued visiting her, and the nurses showed me the chart that required her compliance in daily rehab sessions. They would allow her to stay if my mother followed their directions and complied. There were some improvements, but not enough. The staff was biding their time after the doctor's examination to discharge Mom. The devil was working hard on this whole situation to divert my plans of going to the Holy Land. I prayed in my heart silently to God to make a change in her behavior because I was thinking I should stay and postpone the trip until next year. This was my mother and a good daughter would not leave at a time like this. She needed my emotional support. The situation bothered me so much that it was on my mind constantly. What would I do? My brothers were there; but some men can be less attentive than women. My sister lived in north Florida, miles away.

Everything was in place for the trip. The money was paid in full for both Juliette and me. I discussed my feelings about the trip with Juliette and how going could distress Mom. My daughter understood but left the decision to me. She is a sweet sensitive young lady, and I wanted to experience this trip with her. That Friday night I went to the temple for regular services when a lady walked up to me. She presented me with an envelope and said. "God told me to give this to you". I knew straight away what was in the envelope. It was money, I said to God in my spirit, "Why did you send me money? You knew that I prepared for the trip financially," I placed the envelope in my purse without opening it. When I got home I relaxed for a while and then decided to take a look. In the envelope were fifty Israeli shekels, I knew exactly what to do. I could only spend this money in Israel; He was telling me that it was okay for me to go. This is the kind of relationship I have with my Yeshua and He knew I would understand the message. My Father watches over me. This was not a lot of money, it was just enough to send the message. The Lord knew Mom would recover from her illness and things would get better. I went to Israel and returned to take Mom home from the rehab facility. While I was away my sister–in–law assisted Mom, along with the rest of the family. I had a fabulous spiritual experience in Israel and wished to return the following year. When you have a relationship with Yeshua you will know when He is speaking to you in the Spirit.

The Poem

I love writing, especially if I have something to say. Poetry is just a small part of my script. The only time I had difficulty expressing myself was in writing term papers in college. I laugh when I look back at some papers and why I had to write them. I find pleasure expressing myself though real events which shape my life, making me who I am today. My first real printed material in a book is a poem called "Cry for a People". I started writing little poems in high school, it was mostly rhyming without reason, playing and having fun with girlfriends. They asked for suggestions composing their writings for Valentine's Day or other sweetheart notes to their boyfriends.

Later I was asked to take the position as communication secretary in the church that I attended. My role was to write about all the happenings of the church and report to the general conference. At that time this seemed overwhelming so I refused the position. My best friend Willie encouraged me to take the job. He assured me that he would assist me with writing. I was not good at spelling and I had very poor writing skills which was a deterrent and I still have a lot to learn. He meant what he said and stood by me as I tried to write articles with substance. These were the ones that got accepted into the Magazine for publication. As the years rolled by, I honed my writings skills, and my friend was right there to help me through some difficult times.

I remember one year, I was in church, as usual and was sitting in the pews when I heard my name from the pulpit. The church recognized and awarded me a plaque for consistency in reporting to the conference. This was a surprise as I was not expecting anything because it was my duty. Due to this action my confidence was boosted and I never looked back. As time went by I moved on to another church, that congregation offered me the same position as communication secretary. This time I had experience so I was not afraid.

The church has played a very pivotal role in my writing. It's where I got my start. God had a plan for me, and the church was my training ground. Seeing my articles in print with pictures for the first time was priceless. My church was well represented, and I felt like I was doing what was expected of me. Growing up my parents taught me to work at my job as though God was my employer, giving it my best. I have not been writing for the church for a while and I miss it greatly. Thankfully, the groundwork was already set. I know there was a book inside me and God would help to bring it to light.

In the early days of writing, things would pour out of me like a river. I constantly traveled with a note pad and pencil everywhere I went, because there was always something to write. When my father died, I wanted to write about it then; but it was too painful. However, there was a poem which was forcing its way through my very pores. I felt like this was a commission. I was very angry and upset at the time, losing my Dad; but nothing could stop this reality from pouring out of me. I was working in retail with my degree in electronics; but not doing anything with it. I loved retail, but it was hard and I knew the only way to get out was through education. Moving forward was not an option at the time, so I decided to wait another year or two before pursuing my education. During this time, I had a longing to publish something of my own. The only difference was that I had no control over what I was thinking and feeling to write. I started asking the Lord why I was getting those thoughts and feelings, and why I was so impressed to write. The issue was, deep down in my being a nation is crying out from inside me. This does not make sense; I know that, so allow me to explain. I am Jamaican with no knowledge of who the Jews are. I heard things said about the jewish people, both negative and positive but, it never affected me either way, as I didn't knew or had any affiliation with them. I was taught by my parents to respect all peoples, and the church also instilled common courtesy for all. Living here in the United States allowed me to learn more about different cultures and their backgrounds. I watched documentaries of wars of the world and how they affected lives and people. For the first time, I understood how a group of people can be segregated and destroyed.

When I tried to comprehend this wickendness my reality changed. I saw evil at its worse. It was the early nineties. I had no formal education and high school bearly touched on apartheid. This was the coordination of foundational racial isolation and prejudice that subsisted in South Africa Without any warning and out of nowhere came a force that compelled me to compose this poem "Cry for a People".

CRY FOR A PEOPLE

I CAN HEAR THEM SCREAM WHY DOES IT BOTHER ME SO? THE PAIN, THE FEAR, INCREDIBLE DISBELIEF, I DO NOT KNOW THESE PEOPLE THEY ARE NOT MY RACE, YET SOMETHING DEEP WITHIN ME BURNS, WE ARE JEWS, AND WE ARE A PEOPLE.

HAVE YOU SEEN THE FLAMES? CAN YOU SMELL THE FUMES? IT'S HUMAN FLESH, PILES AND PILES OF THEM, NAKED, SKELETON ALMOST. BOMB THE FURNACES, CUT OPEN THE FENCES, FREEDOM IS CALLING, FAINT, SLOW, AND, FAR AWAY. WERE WE ALL BLIND? NO ONE CAME TO HELP; THEY TOOK OUR DIGNITY, PRIDE AND SHAME. WHAT HAVE YOU ACHIEVED? WHERE IS YOUR GAIN?

COULD EVIL RISE AGAIN? I WONDER WHAT IT TAKES. TEN BILLION PEOPLE STRONG? TONS AND TONS OF WEAPONS? NO, NOT MUCH. JUST CLOSE YOUR EYES, TURN YOUR HEADS, AND GENTLY LOOK AWAY.

When I was writing this poem, I asked myself why I never wrote about Africa and slavery. The answer came straight away. I was not impressed to do so, it's that simple. Today when I read this poem, I see myself embedded in the words, being a part of the questioning and answering at the same time.

God says we must love each other like ourselves. He said we must love Him first them each other (Deuteronomy 6:4-5).

I could not explain the passion, but it is okay. I thank God that He placed a love in my heart for all nations, tongues, and people. I will continue to write, but only for Yeshua. May His worship continuously be on my lips, and my mouth shall always shout His praises.

A Partner

I have had many disappointments with relationships trying to find the perfect husband. After two failed marriages, I tried dating again. My search brought me to different online dating sites, where the most dysfunctional individuals hang out hoping for suitable matches. Others were there to prey upon the vulnerability of unsuspecting women desperate for loving companionships. I remember a seemingly kind-hearted well-spoken engineer requesting money from me in less than a week. My search ended following a match from Texas who claimed to be a Christian. This person had all the criteria for which I was looking. He was a Bible-believing man of God. He came to see me in beautiful Ft. Lauderdale, Florida, where I picked him up at the airport and took him to his hotel. In my spirit, I felt that he was not the one; but friends and family encouraged me to take a chance. This was some time after my failed engagement, so I was very cautious and leery.

He appeared pleasant and happy. We talked about our children and exchanged pictures. He told me how his wife left him with the kids, and his family was helping by giving loving support. I gathered that he was looking for a wife and mother and I was a good match. His visit came at a time when I was on vacation form work, so I had the opportunity to spend time knowing who he really was. Our time together included visits to the beach, where we walked along the shores. We enjoyed parks, and movies. At church, I introduced him to a few of my friends and they seemed to like him. One of my brothers took us fishing and cooked what we caught for dinner. The fellowship was great and the days that followed were just as pleasant.

I should have listened to God when He tried to warn me that this man was going to be a great disappointment. I was getting ready to visit my aunt in Jamaica when he made contact with me via social media. We were texting for two weeks before that and just before leaving, he asked me to allow him to accompany me there. I felt concerned that it was too soon because he did not know me well enough. Visiting with family in Jamaica is always amazing. I spend the best time with my cousins and loving aunt. They take me to some of the most beautiful places on the Island. Historic Port Royal for lunch, the white sandy beaches in the parish of Portland, shopping at the malls in New Kingston, and so much more amenities, my vacations are always splendid. My contact with this individual through social media continued. Let's call him George. He texted me while I was there, and we made plans to meet up in Florida when I returned from Jamaica. I told him that I wanted to fast about everything, including our meeting. He decided to do the same.

A Partner

George's profile stated that he lived in Texas and claimed to be an engineer seeking companionship. I chose to believe him. That Sabbath morning, I went to church and fasted until 4:00 p.m. The following morning, not hearing from him, I went to the computer to see if he posted or texted me. A full screen came up detailing George seeking girls from the age of eighteen through forty-four. The time and date on the computer was current. I could not believe my eyes. My concern was that we were supposed to be doing this spiritual fasting and staying away from the dating scene since we had connected. The deception was telling. I made contact with him and confronted him on the fact that he was planning a meeting date with me while seeking others. I knew already that it was time to walk away. Through fasting and prayer, God answered me and showed me his true character and I could not deny the revelation. This might seem strange; but the year 1844 was a time in the Adventist history when they believed God would have returned but it did not happen. Today that event is called the Great Disappointment. I knew this because I was a Seventh Day Adventist before I converted to the Messianic faith. George told me that he meant nothing by it and that he still wanted to meet with me.

After I got home, friends and family convinced me to forgive him and that it was probably nothing. The time came for me to pick him up at the airport. We had dinner, and he was pleasant and appeared to be happy that we met. The following few days were exciting for me because I had not been dating anyone. I enjoyed the company of a believer, or so I thought, it was interesting and lovely. We never once studied the Word (Bible) or discussed anything spiritual, this was strange to me. My greatest joy is to have a partner who loves the Lord, and is willing to study the Word of God and worship as a couple.

The following day was his departure date so we planned to have a wonderful dinner together and say our good-byes. We went back to the hotel, where he invited me for a swim. I refused because I had no swim-suit and I was uncomfortable going into the pool at night with an individual I had known for just a few days. He insisted by offering me one of his t-shirts to swim in, and I respectfully declined. I believe this was how George operated. He visited these ladies he meets online, wines and dines them, takes the best of what they have to offer and leaves, never to return. The following day, he was not as accommodating to me. I took him back to the airport, where he left with just a good-bye.

When he went back to Texas, he called for some information, which I provided. Because he told me of his upcoming baptism that following Saturday, I called to congratulate him and wished him well. After that call there was no further interaction between us. I missed the fun we had and I hurt to know that precious time was wasted talking about personal life experiences for nothing. The weeks that followed proved to be more unbelievable for my brother, he called George without a response. They had such a great time fishing together, how could this person be so cold?

God's plans are perfect and sure. When He puts things in place, they come to pass. We must depend on Yeshua for everything. Without Him our plans will surely fail every time. One month passed and I started to forget the experience. I had moved on. Then I saw an email from George asking about some old story that happened in Port Royal Jamaica regarding the great earthquake of June 7, 1692. The email was fluffy, light, and almost playful. I tried to ignore it but I answered. I asked him not to text me as if we were friends. I told him that he was inconsiderate of my feelings and what he did was very unkind. He did not have an excuse and after all that time, I really did not care to know. I told him never to text, call, or email me in the future. His apology was weak, and we never communicated again.

Well, I had enough. I promised the Lord that I would wait for His hand in my life. Unless He chose for me I would remain single — no more dating. By God's grace I have the strength to wait on the Lord. I had been waiting for more than eight years, not dating anyone, keeping my promise to the God that I love, the best companion an individual can have. Bless the name Yeshua.

Mother's Day 2020 was three weeks away and I received a call from my daughter and her husband Thomas, inviting me to Animal Kingdom in Orlando for a Mother's Day gift. I declined the invitation even though I wanted to go because I felt like a bother being the third wheel. My daughter guilted me into going, she claimed that it was her Mother's day gift and I should accept it. Uncle Scotty, a gentleman and friend they knew also wanted to go. Before the trip I was not feeling well, and this alone would normally stop me from going; but my daughter wanted me to experience the Avatar animation. We watched the movie and loved it, that featured attraction was even better, especially the vertual ride. There was one stop at Scott's place in Jupiter, Florida before moving on to Orlando. When we got there, everyone boarded a bigger vehicle. The luggage was loaded as well. As I reached for mine, Scott asked to take my luggage (which was not too heavy for me) but I gave it to him. Something about that action was kind and it made me feel more comfortable going.

The ride was calm, peaceful, and the beautiful landscaping went on for miles. Everyone was in a good mood. The atmosphere was light and we were enjoying the music playing on the radio. When we arrived in Orlando, we went to the line for the Avatar ride immediately. There were hundreds of people waiting to get in, the sun was hot; but we were anticipating the ride, which promised to be once in a lifetime. The wait was two hours long, Scott was mostly on his phone and Juliette and Thomas chatted together. I occupied my time by taking in the surroundings which depicted the Avatar life in the trees. A few times Scott and I exchanged pleasantries; but he soon went back to his phone and I to my sightseeing.

The ride was amazing, I felt like we were in a different world, the colors were more brilliant, the animals and trees seemed bigger. I rode one of the dragons and got scared because of the height. After the ride, I found out that Scott and I had the same issue with the height and were both dizzy from the shaking, tumbling, and rolling during the virtual trip. At the close of the day we went to dinner at a cozy little restaurant. The food was delicious. We laughed and discussed the day's events. We were about finish when it started raining. During the meal, Scott and I spoke some more about generalities, he seemed a bit distracted but polite. When it was time to go, Scott tried to shelter me from the rain by pulling the vehicle closer to the curb which was successful.

Later that evening we went to the cabin, where we watched a movie and relaxed for a while. Just like that Scott asked to take my blood pressure. He had his machine and vitamins on the table in plain sight. This person was open and honest I said to myself. I thought it was a bit forward since I did not tell him that I was hypertensive. So you can imagine my surprise when he made his request. I humbly sat down and he did the honors. My pressure was a bit high and he offered to give me pointers on keeping it lower. As the night progressed, he started talking to me about his life experiences and I knew that he felt trusting and safe expressing himself to me. I listened intently without interruption. He wanted to talk and I was prepared to listen. Actually, I am a counselor and know how to listen. We must have communicated for a very long time because we were the only ones still awake. He thanked me for listening and told me how much he appreciated the time we spent just talking.

The next morning he got breakfast for everyone, coffee and donuts; but I love hot chocolate, which he promised to get next time. It was time to leave for home and God gave me a song. It played over and over again in my mind. I had to share it with everyone. It's called "Thank *you for the Cross Lord" so* when we got into the car I asked Scott to play it, as he was the designated driver home. He said there was a favorite he had planned on playing first, so we listened and worshipped after which he played mine.

In less than two minutes, I heard him say "Wow" and I looked up to see the biggest cross ever, planted on the side of the road. This cross was so big that it could be seen from miles away. It was built like a highway sign but much taller. I worshipped even more because I knew it was not a coincidence. God was with us and we had a lovely safe ride back to the apartment. The day was still young so we decided to have some fun playing card games. I had the perfect one called donkey; my brothers and I played it a lot because it's full of laughs. Scott was hesitant about playing; he did not know this game or the name of it. After a few prompts from everyone he gave in. The whole idea of the game was to lay all the cards down quietly, after finding your entire match, and not being the last to do so if others found theirs before you. Scott was the last to lay his cards down on six occasions, so he ended up being the donkey.

We laughed so much that it was hard to catch our breath. He was a good sport and furthermore he was just learning the game. Overall the trip turned out to be great!! I had an enjoyable time. Scott decided to call and give Thomas the information for suppressing my blood pressure, as promised. I told him he could give it to me directly via phone when he was ready. I felt at ease with that.

The phone rang that same night and I knew it was Scott. He gave me the information and we chatted for a long time about everything and nothing. It felt wonderful to talk to someone who had the same spiritual convictions and who loved the Lord. This was strange to me. He had been attending the Mishkan David temple for ten years during this time, but he never saw me. I had been going there for more than seven years and I never saw him. He had a relationship with Thomas and my daughter for years. They affectionately called him Uncle Scotty; I heard of him but never met him.

At the temple, he would smile at me or come over to meet and greet; but we were low-keyed and private. A couple of Shabbat following, a woman approached me and told me that my husband was coming. She said God placed it on her heart and I would meet him soon. I laughed, thanked her, and walked away. She did it again the next Shabbat, even describing his personality. It sounded very much like Scott. She asked me if I already met him as she was so sure of his arrival. More individuals started telling me the same thing. I did not tell Scott about these encounters because God has a way of working things out. He will know soon enough. I told my daughter that Scott and I had been communicating and enjoyed the idea of becoming more acquainted. She and her Thomas were happy about that because they loved "Uncle Scotty".

It was more than a month since our first meeting and Scott wanted to know my age. The next time he asked me, I told him to guess. His reply was priceless, with a funny smile on his face he said, "I don't want to be the donkey twice." We laughed so hard that I could not contain myself. By this time I was very attracted to Scott and he felt the same about me. We prayed and sang together on the phone. He plays the guitar and sings very well and that is very appealing to me. We knew we belonged together so it was time to tell our close family and the Rabbi, which we did. A wedding date was set for later that year; but a fear came over me and I started thinking negatively. I remembered all the poor choices I made in the past. God was my only source of comfort. He would tell me what to do, so I asked Him how to navigate things. I shared my insecurities, doubts, and fears with Him, not holding anything back because I felt like this was it. The following week a friend of mine that sang with me in the choir came running to me with something into her hand. She said God reminded her three times to give it to me. It was a CD with a lady dressed in bridal attire on the cover. When I saw it my confirmation came. God knows everything. "He counts the number of stars, He gives name to all of them, great is our Lord, and abundant in power, His knowledge is infinite" (Psalm 147:4-5). I had confidence that this person was to be my husband. We are now married and living in God's love and grace. Trusting Yeshua is the best thing I have ever done; my life is changed for the better and yours can too. God is our Father, we are His children and it is His desire to bless us. Turn over your life to Him and watch Him transform you into who He wants you to be shalom.

www.ingramcontent.com/pod-product-compliance
Ingram Content Group UK Ltd.
Pitfield, Milton Keynes, MK11 3LW, UK
UKHW022216230426
12048UKWH00016BA/879